The MongoDB Cheat Sheet

A 3-Hours Practical Guide with Essential Tips and Tricks

Published by : Kumar Abhiii

Copyright

The MongoDB Cheat Sheet: A 3-Hours Practical Guide with Essential Tips and Tricks

First Edition, 2024

Published by Kumar Abhiii

Dedication

To all the learners, developers, and database enthusiasts who seek to improve their skills and make MongoDB a powerful tool in their development journey. This book is dedicated to you for your commitment to learning and growing.

Acknowledgments

I would like to extend my deepest gratitude to my family, friends, and supporters who have encouraged me throughout this journey. A special thanks to the MongoDB community for providing endless resources, inspiration, and learning. I would also like to thank all the developers and database administrators who have contributed to the continued growth of MongoDB. Lastly, a big thank you to all the learners who will benefit from this book—you are the true motivation behind this work.

Thank you all!

Preface

Welcome to *The MongoDB Cheat Sheet: A 3-Hours Practical Guide with Essential Tips and Tricks* This guide was created with one goal in mind: to provide you with an easy-to-use reference for learning and mastering MongoDB quickly and effectively. Whether you're a beginner looking to get started or an experienced developer needing quick tips and tricks, this book is designed to give you the knowledge you need in a short amount of time.

In this practical guide, you'll find clear explanations, hands-on examples, and key MongoDB commands that will help you master the basics and explore advanced features. Each section is crafted to offer quick insights and to-the-point instructions, making it the perfect resource for developers who need fast answers and want to improve their MongoDB skills on the go.

~ Kumar Abhiii

About the Author

Kumar Abhiii (Abhishek Parmar) is the founder of 9xcode.com, a passionate technology educator, professional software engineer, and author. With years of experience in the tech industry, he is committed to helping students and professionals achieve their career goals by making complex concepts easy to understand and apply.

As an accomplished book author with works published on Amazon, Abhiii takes a practical, hands-on approach to teaching, using real-world examples to ensure learners not only grasp the material but also retain and apply it for long-term success.

For more learning resources, visit: https://9xcode.com/

Table of Contents

Chapter 1: Introduction to MongoDB

What is MongoDB?

MongoDB is a NoSQL database that stores data in flexible, JSON-like documents instead of tables. This makes it ideal for handling large volumes of unstructured data. It's scalable, fast, and designed for modern applications that require flexibility and real-time data access.

Key Features and Benefits

- **Scalable**: MongoDB scales horizontally across multiple servers.
- **Flexible Schema**: No fixed schema required, allowing diverse data types in the same collection.
- **High Performance**: Optimized for fast queries and large datasets.
- **Easy to Use**: Uses a query language similar to JavaScript.

Basic Concepts: Databases, Collections, Documents

- **Databases**: Containers for collections. Each database is separate.
- **Collections**: Groups of documents, similar to tables in relational databases.
- **Documents**: The basic unit of data, stored in BSON format (Binary JSON).

Example: A blog post document might look like this:

```
{

    "_id": ObjectId("..."),

    "title": "Understanding MongoDB",

    "author": "John Doe",

    "content": "MongoDB is a NoSQL
database..."

}
```

Chapter 2: Setting Up MongoDB

Installing MongoDB (Local and Cloud)

1. **Local Installation**:

   - Download MongoDB from the official website (https://www.mongodb.com/try/download/community).
   - Follow the installation steps for your operating system (Windows, macOS, or Linux).
   - Start the MongoDB server by running **mongod**.

2. **Cloud Installation**:

   - Sign up for a free cluster on MongoDB Atlas (https://www.mongodb.com/atlas).
   - Create a new cluster and follow the guided steps to set it up.
   - Use the provided connection string to access your cluster.

Connecting to MongoDB

Local Connection:

Use the MongoDB Shell (**mongosh**) to connect to your local database:

```
mongosh
```

Cloud Connection:

Replace **<username>**, **<password>**, and **<cluster-url>** in the connection string provided by Atlas:

```
mongosh
"mongodb+srv://<username>:<password>@<cluste
r-url>/test"
```

MongoDB Shell Basics

The MongoDB shell (**mongosh**) is an interactive interface to interact with your database. Here are some basic commands:

Show Databases:

Lists all databases.

```
show dbs
```

Use a Database:

Switches to (or creates) a database named **myDatabase**.

```
use myDatabase
```

Show Collections:

Lists all collections in the current database.

```
show collections
```

Insert a Document:

To add a document to a collection, use **insertOne**

```
db.myCollection.insertOne({ name: "John",
age: 30 })
```

Query a Collection:

To find documents where the age is greater than 25, run:

```
db.myCollection.find({ age: { $gt: 25 } })
```

Chapter 3: Core Data Operations (CRUD)

MongoDB's CRUD operations — **Create**, **Read**, **Update**, and **Delete** — are essential for working with any database. Let's explore these operations with clear examples and real-world scenarios.

Insert: Adding Documents to Collections

To add a document to a MongoDB collection, use **insertOne** or **insertMany** for single or multiple documents.

Example

Adding a single user to a **users** collection:

```
db.users.insertOne({ name: "Alice", age: 25,
email: "alice@example.com" })
```

To add multiple users:

```
db.users.insertMany([
```

```
  { name: "Bob", age: 30, email:
"bob@example.com" },

  { name: "Carol", age: 28, email:
"carol@example.com" }

])
```

Query: Finding Documents with Filters

Use **find** to retrieve documents from a collection. You can filter results using query operators.

Example

Finding all users aged above 25:

```
db.users.find({ age: { $gt: 25 } })
```

To retrieve only specific fields, use projections. Example: Fetching only names and emails:

```
db.users.find({}, { name: 1, email: 1, _id:
0 })
```

Update: Modifying Existing Documents

Update documents using **updateOne**, **updateMany**, or **replaceOne**.

Example

Updating a user's email by their name:

```
db.users.updateOne(

  { name: "Alice" },

  { $set: { email: "alice.new@example.com" }
}

)
```

Updating multiple users:

```
db.users.updateMany(

  { age: { $lt: 30 } },

  { $inc: { age: 1 } }

)
```

Delete: Removing Documents

Delete documents using **deleteOne** or **deleteMany**.

Example

Removing a single user by name:

```
db.users.deleteOne({ name: "Bob" })
```

Removing all users aged under 25:

```
db.users.deleteMany({ age: { $lt: 25 } })
```

Chapter 4: Working with Queries

MongoDB provides powerful query capabilities to retrieve and manipulate data effectively. This chapter covers common query operators, result modifications, and working with arrays and embedded documents.

Basic Query Operators

Query operators allow you to filter data based on specific conditions. Here are some commonly used ones:

Equality ($eq): Matches documents where a field equals a value.

Example: Finding users aged 30:

```
db.users.find({ age: { $eq: 30 } })
```

Greater Than ($gt) and Less Than ($lt): Filters based on numerical comparisons.

Example: Finding users older than 25:

```
db.users.find({ age: { $gt: 25 } })
```

In ($in): Matches any value in an array of possibilities.

Example: Finding users aged 25, 30, or 35:

```
db.users.find({ age: { $in: [25, 30,
35] } })
```

Sorting, Limiting, and Projecting Results

To organize and refine query results, MongoDB offers sorting, limiting, and projections.

Sorting: Use **sort** to order results.

Example: Sorting users by age in ascending order:

```
db.users.find().sort({ age: 1 })
```

Limiting: Use **limit** to restrict the number of returned results.

Example: Fetching only the first 3 users:

```
db.users.find().limit(3)
```

Projecting: Use **projections** to return specific fields.

Example: Fetching only names and emails:

```
db.users.find({}, { name: 1, email: 1, _id:
0 })
```

Filtering Arrays and Embedded Documents

MongoDB allows you to query arrays and embedded documents with precision.

Filtering Arrays:

Example: Finding users who like "coding":

```
db.users.find({ hobbies: "coding" })
```

Example: Users with more than two hobbies:

```
db.users.find({ hobbies: { $size: 3 } })
```

Embedded Documents: Use dot notation to access fields within embedded documents.

Example: Finding users who live in New York:

```
db.users.find({ "address.city": "New York" })
```

Chapter 5: Indexes

Indexes are essential for improving query performance in MongoDB. They allow the database to quickly locate data, reducing the need for scanning entire collections.

Why Indexes Matter

Indexes significantly enhance query speed by narrowing down the search space. Without indexes, MongoDB performs a **collection scan**, which checks every document, leading to slower performance for large datasets.

Example: Searching for a user by name without an index: The query will scan every document in the collection, even if only a few match the criteria.

With an index, MongoDB can jump directly to the relevant data, making queries faster and more efficient.

Creating and Using Indexes

To create an index, use the **createIndex** method. Here's how to create and utilize indexes:

Single Field Index:

Index a single field to optimize queries filtering by that field.

Example: Creating an index on the **name** field:

```
db.users.createIndex({ name: 1 })
```

The **1** specifies ascending order; use **-1** for descending order.

Using the Index:

When you query a collection with a field that has an index, MongoDB uses the index to fetch results faster. Example:

```
db.users.find({ name: "Alice" })
```

Common Index Types

Single Field Index:

Indexes one field for basic queries. Example: Searching by **email**:

```
db.users.createIndex({ email: 1 })
```

Compound Index:

Indexes multiple fields for combined queries. Example: Optimizing queries filtering by **name** and sorting by **age**:

```
db.users.createIndex({ name: 1, age: -1 })
```

Text Index:

Enables text search within string fields. Example: Creating a text index on the **bio** field:

```
db.users.createIndex({ bio: "text" })
```

Querying with a text index:

```
db.users.find({ $text: { $search:
"developer" } })
```

Chapter 6: Aggregation Basics

MongoDB's **aggregation framework** allows you to process data in a more advanced way than simple queries. It helps you group, filter, and transform data with greater flexibility, making it essential for data analysis and reporting.

Understanding the Aggregation Pipeline

The aggregation pipeline processes data through multiple stages. Each stage transforms the data, and the result from one stage is passed to the next.

Example:

```
db.orders.aggregate([

  { $match: { status: "completed" } },

  { $group: { _id: "$customerId",
totalAmount: { $sum: "$amount" } } },

  { $sort: { totalAmount: -1 } }

])
```

Key Stages

$match: Filters documents based on conditions.
Example:

```
{ $match: { status: "completed" } }
```

$group: Groups documents and performs calculations.
Example:

```
{ $group: { _id: "$customerId", totalAmount:
{ $sum: "$amount" } } }
```

$sort: Sorts documents by a field.
Example:

```
{ $sort: { totalAmount: -1 } }
```

$project: Selects fields to include or exclude.
Example:

```
{ $project: { _id: 1, totalAmount: 1 } }
```

Sample Aggregation Queries

Total Sales by Customer:

```
db.orders.aggregate([

   { $group: { _id: "$customerId",
totalSales: { $sum: "$amount" } } }

])
```

Find Orders in a Date Range:

```
db.orders.aggregate([

   { $match: { orderDate: { $gte:
ISODate("2024-01-01"), $lte: ISODate("2024-
12-31") } } }

])
```

Top Products by Sales:

```
db.orders.aggregate([

   { $group: { _id: "$productId", totalSales:
{ $sum: "$amount" } } },

   { $sort: { totalSales: -1 } },

   { $limit: 5 }

])
```

Chapter 7: Schema Design Best Practices

Designing an efficient schema is essential for performance and scalability in MongoDB. The flexibility of MongoDB allows you to model your data according to your application's requirements.

Embedded vs. Referenced Data Models

Embedded Data Model

Store related data together in the same document.

Use Case: When related data is frequently accessed together.

Example:

```
{
  "orderId": 123,
  "customer": {
    "name": "John Doe",
    "email": "john@example.com"
```

```
  },
  "items": [
    { "productId": "p1", "quantity": 2 },
    { "productId": "p2", "quantity": 1 }
  ]
}
```

Referenced Data Model

Store related data in separate collections and link them with references.

Use Case: When related data is large or frequently updated independently.

Example

```
{
  "orderId": 123,
  "customerId": "c1",
  "items": ["i1", "i2"]
}
```

Tips for Efficient Schema Design

1. **Understand Your Queries:** Design your schema around the queries your application will run most frequently.

2. **Minimize Joins:** Prefer embedding to avoid expensive joins unless data size or update frequency suggests referencing.

3. **Keep Document Size in Check:** MongoDB has a document size limit of 16 MB. Split large documents when necessary.

4. **Use Indexes Wisely:** Create indexes on fields frequently used in queries to improve read performance.

Common Patterns

Bucket Pattern: Used to store time-series or event data by grouping related entries into "buckets."

Example: Store daily sensor readings in a single document

```
{

  "sensorId": "s1",

  "date": "2024-11-17",

  "readings": [

    { "time": "10:00", "value": 25 },

    { "time": "11:00", "value": 30 }

  ]

}
```

Outlier Pattern: Separate frequently accessed "hot" data from infrequently accessed "cold" data to optimize performance.

Attribute Pattern: Flatten nested fields into key-value pairs for flexible querying.

Example

```
{

  "productId": "p1",

  "attributes": {

    "color": "red",

    "size": "M"

  }

}
```

Chapter 8: Advanced Topics (Quick Overview)

This chapter provides a high-level overview of essential advanced MongoDB features that help improve availability, scalability, and data consistency.

Replication: High Availability and Failover

Replication ensures data redundancy and availability by synchronizing data across multiple servers.

- **Replica Set**: A group of MongoDB servers that maintain the same data. One server acts as the **primary**, while others are **secondaries**.
- **Failover**: If the primary server fails, a secondary automatically takes over as the new primary.

Benefits:

- High availability during server failures.
- Data redundancy for disaster recovery.

Example Command:

```
rs.initiate({

  _id: "replicaSetName",

  members: [

    { _id: 0, host: "primaryHost:27017" },

    { _id: 1, host:
"secondaryHost1:27017" },

    { _id: 2, host: "secondaryHost2:27017" }

  ]

})
```

Sharding: Scaling with Large Data

Sharding allows you to horizontally scale your database
by distributing data across multiple servers.

- **Shard Key**: A field used to distribute data evenly
  across shards.
- **Components**:
    - **Config Servers**: Store metadata and cluster
      configuration.
    - **Shard Servers**: Store data.
    - **Query Routers (mongos)**: Route queries to
      appropriate shards.

Benefits:

- Handle large datasets efficiently.
- Distribute write operations across servers.

Example Command:

```
sh.enableSharding("myDatabase")

sh.shardCollection("myDatabase.myCollection"
, { shardKey: 1 })
```

Transactions: Working with Multiple Documents

Transactions in MongoDB provide **ACID** guarantees for operations across multiple documents and collections.

When to Use:

- Banking systems: Updating balances in multiple accounts.
- E-commerce: Placing an order while reducing inventory stock.

Example: (javascript code)

```
const session =
db.getMongo().startSession();
```

```
const ordersCollection =
session.getDatabase("myDatabase").orders;

const inventoryCollection =
session.getDatabase("myDatabase").inventory;


session.startTransaction();

try {

  ordersCollection.insertOne({ orderId: 123,
status: "placed" });

  inventoryCollection.updateOne({ productId:
"p1" }, { $inc: { stock: -1 } });

  session.commitTransaction();

} catch (error) {

  session.abortTransaction();

}

session.endSession();
```

Chapter 9: Security Essentials

Securing your MongoDB deployment is crucial to protecting your data and ensuring that only authorized users have access. This chapter provides a quick guide to MongoDB's core security features.

Basic Authentication and Authorization

Authentication verifies the identity of users, while authorization ensures they can only access what they're allowed to.

Steps to Enable Authentication:

1. Create an Admin User:

```
use admin

db.createUser({

  user: "adminUser",

  pwd: "strongPassword",

  roles: ["root"]

})
```

2. Enable Authentication in the Configuration File: Edit the **mongod.conf** file to include

```
security:

  authorization: "enabled"
```

3. Restart the MongoDB Service:

```
sudo systemctl restart mongod
```

Role-Based Access Control (RBAC)

RBAC assigns specific roles to users, limiting what actions they can perform. MongoDB includes predefined roles, or you can create custom roles.

Common Built-In Roles:

- **Read**: Allows read-only access to a database.
- **ReadWrite**: Allows read and write operations.
- **dbAdmin**: Allows administrative tasks like indexing and statistics.
- **ClusterAdmin**: For managing the cluster and monitoring.

Example: Creating a Read-Write User

```
use myDatabase

db.createUser({

  user: "appUser",

  pwd: "appPassword",

  roles: [{ role: "readWrite", db:
"myDatabase" }]

})
```

Tips for Securing Your MongoDB Deployment

1. **Use Strong Passwords**: Ensure all users have complex, unique passwords.

2. **Bind MongoDB to Localhost**: By default, MongoDB listens on **localhost**. For production, configure it to limit access to specific Ips.

```
net:

  bindIp: 127.0.0.1
```

3. **Enable TLS/SSL**: Encrypt data in transit by enabling TLS

```
mongod --sslMode requireSSL --
sslPEMKeyFile /path/to/ssl.pem
```

4. **Monitor Activity**: Use tools like MongoDB Cloud Manager to track database activity and detect anomalies.

5. **Limit Network Exposure**: Deploy MongoDB behind a firewall or VPN and avoid exposing it directly to the internet.

Chapter 10: Administration and Maintenance

Effective administration and maintenance ensure your MongoDB deployment runs smoothly and remains reliable over time. This chapter covers essential tasks like backups, performance monitoring, and common admin commands.

Backups and Restores

Regular backups protect your data from unexpected failures or human errors.

Backing Up with mongodump: Creates a backup of your database in BSON format

```
mongodump --db=myDatabase
-out=/backup/location
```

Restoring with mongorestore: Reimports data from a backup created by mongodump.

```
mongorestore --db=myDatabase
/backup/location/myDatabase
```

Monitoring Performance

Monitoring helps identify performance bottlenecks and optimize resource usage.

Tools for Monitoring:

1. **MongoDB Compass**: Provides a GUI for monitoring query performance and schema analysis.
2. **MongoDB Atlas**: Includes built-in monitoring for metrics like CPU, memory, and I/O usage.
3. **Database Profiler**: Tracks slow queries for optimization.

Enable the Profiler:

```
db.setProfilingLevel(1) // Logs slow
operations
```

Check Slow Queries:

```
db.system.profile.find({ millis: { $gt:
100 } }) // Queries taking >100ms
```

Common Commands for Admin Tasks

Here are some frequently used commands for database management:

Check Server Status:

```
db.serverStatus()
```

View Active Connections:

```
db.currentOp()
```

Rebuild Indexes:

```
db.collectionName.reIndex()
```

Compact a Collection: Reduces storage size for a collection.

```
db.runCommand({ compact: "collectionName" })
```

View Disk Usage:

```
db.stats()
```

Chapter 11: Quick Reference Guide

This chapter serves as a handy cheat sheet for frequently used MongoDB commands, syntax, and practical tips to streamline your workflow.

Key MongoDB Commands Cheat Sheet

1. **Database Management**:

   - Show all databases: **show dbs**
   - Switch or create a database: **use myDatabase**
   - Drop a database: **db.dropDatabase()**

2. **Collection Management**:

   - List collections in the current database: **show collections**
   - Create a collection: **db.createCollection("myCollection")**
   - Drop a collection: **db.myCollection.drop()**

3. **CRUD Operations**:

- Insert a document:

  db.myCollection.insertOne({ name: "John", age: 30 })

- Query documents:

  db.myCollection.find({ age: { $gt: 20 } })

- Update a document:

  db.myCollection.updateOne({ name: "John" }, { $set: { age: 31 } })

- Delete a document:

  db.myCollection.deleteOne({ name: "John" })

4. **Index Management**:

- Create an index:

  db.myCollection.createIndex({ name: 1 })

- View indexes:

  db.myCollection.getIndexes()

- Drop an index:

  db.myCollection.dropIndex("name_1")

5. **Performance and Stats**:

- Check collection statistics:

  db.myCollection.stats()

- Enable database profiler:

  db.setProfilingLevel(2)

Common MongoDB Syntax and Tips

1. **Query Operators**:

- Equality: **$eq**
  Example: **db.myCollection.find({ age: { $eq: 30 } })**
- Greater than: **$gt**
  Example: **db.myCollection.find({ age: { $gt: 20 } })**
- In an array: **$in**
  Example: **db.myCollection.find({ name: { $in: ["Alice", "Bob"] } })**

2. **Projection**:

- Include specific fields:
  db.myCollection.find({}, { name: 1, age: 1 })

3. **Aggregation Pipeline**:

- Simple aggregation example:
  db.myCollection.aggregate([{ $match: { age: { $gte: 20 } } }, { $group: { _id: "$age", count: { $sum: 1 } } }])

4. **Tips for Efficiency**:

- Always use indexes for frequently queried fields.
- Avoid large **$or** queries; refactor into smaller **$in** queries where possible.
- Limit data returned by queries to save memory:

db.myCollection.find({}).limit(10)

Thank You and Congratulations!

Congratulations on completing *The MongoDB Cheat Sheet: A 3-Hours Practical Guide with Essential Tips and Tricks*

We hope this book has equipped you with the practical skills to confidently work with MongoDB. From the basics to advanced topics, you now have the tools to build, optimize, and secure your databases.

This guide was designed to help you learn quickly, with clear examples you can apply to your projects. Whether you're a beginner or refreshing your skills, we aimed to make this a practical reference.

Thank you for choosing this guide. We're excited to see how you apply your new MongoDB knowledge to your projects and career.

If you found this book helpful, please consider leaving a review and sharing it with others. Your feedback helps others discover this resource.

For more learning, check out our other book, Bun.js in Action: Real-World Solutions for Building Modern Backends, which covers fast, scalable backends using modern technologies.

For more learning resources and updates, visit: https://9xcode.com/

Happy coding,
Kumar Abhiii

www.ingramcontent.com/pod-product-compliance
Lightning Source LLC
LaVergne TN
LVHW051751050326
832903LV00029B/2848